Best Handwriting
for ages 6-7

We hope that you enjoy working through this book.

If you are right-handed you should hold your pencil like this.
If you are left-handed you should hold your pencil like this.

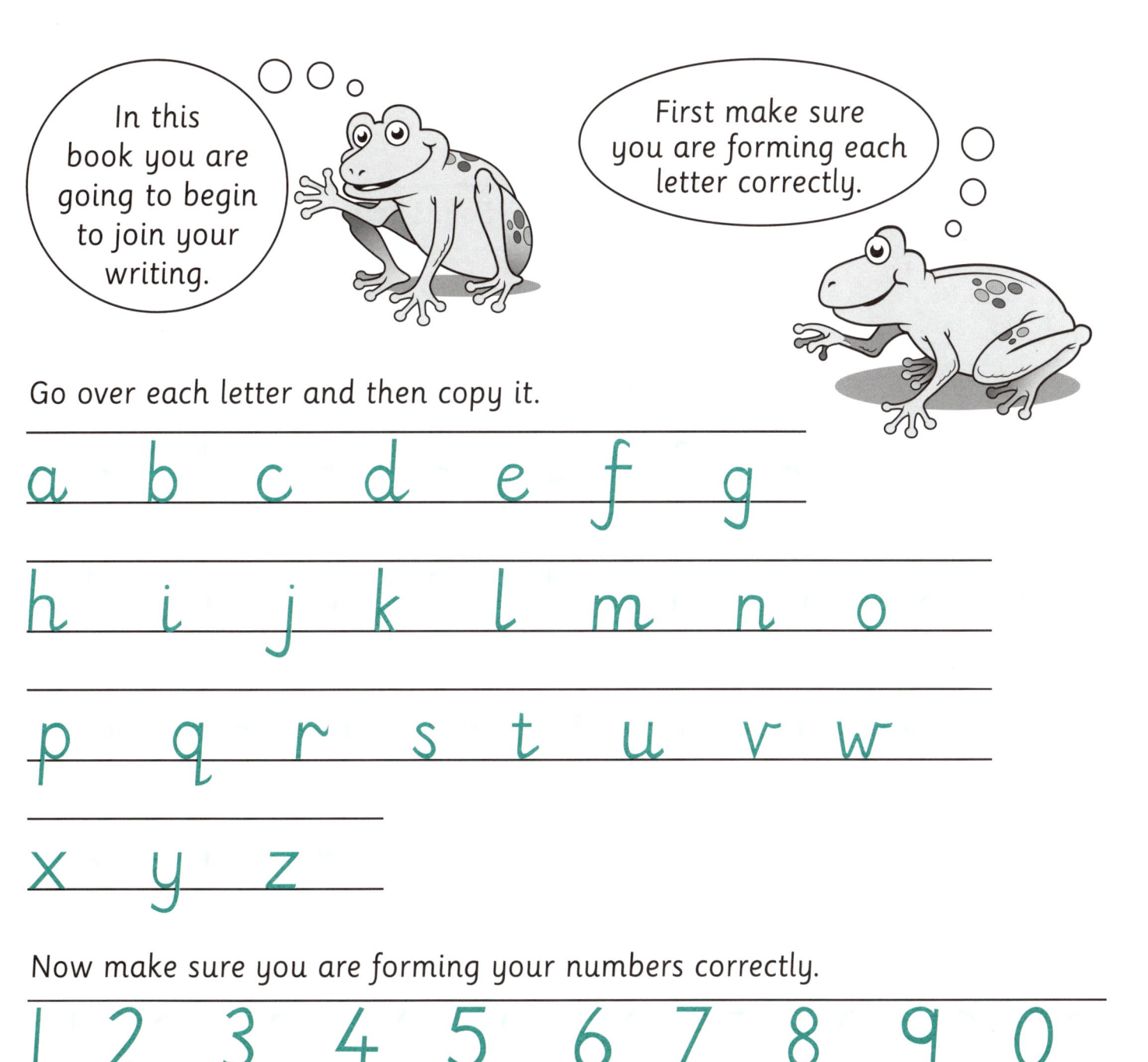

In this book you are going to begin to join your writing.

First make sure you are forming each letter correctly.

Go over each letter and then copy it.

a b c d e f g

h i j k l m n o

p q r s t u v w

x y z

Now make sure you are forming your numbers correctly.

1 2 3 4 5 6 7 8 9 0

We are going to join some pairs of letters.

Points to remember
- Keep your letters the right size.
- Work slowly and carefully.
- Do not press too hard on the paper.

Go over my joined letters and then try your own.

ai   ai   ai   ai   *ae   ae   ae   ae*

am   am   am   *an   an   an   an*

ar   ar   ar   ar   *as   as   as   as*

✏️ The joining line goes from the bottom of the first letter to the top of the next so we call this a slope join.

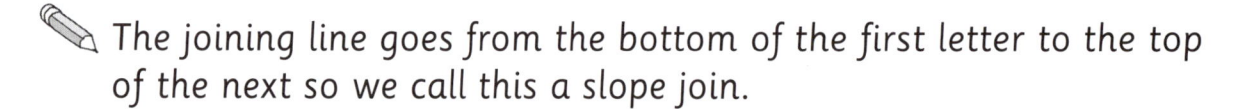

Now try joining these letters.

Remember to work slowly and carefully.

ea ea ea ea   ei ei ei ei

en en en en   eu eu eu eu

ec ec ec ec   eo eo eo eo

ee ee ee ee   er er er er

Look at this join.

ca

Now try it yourself.

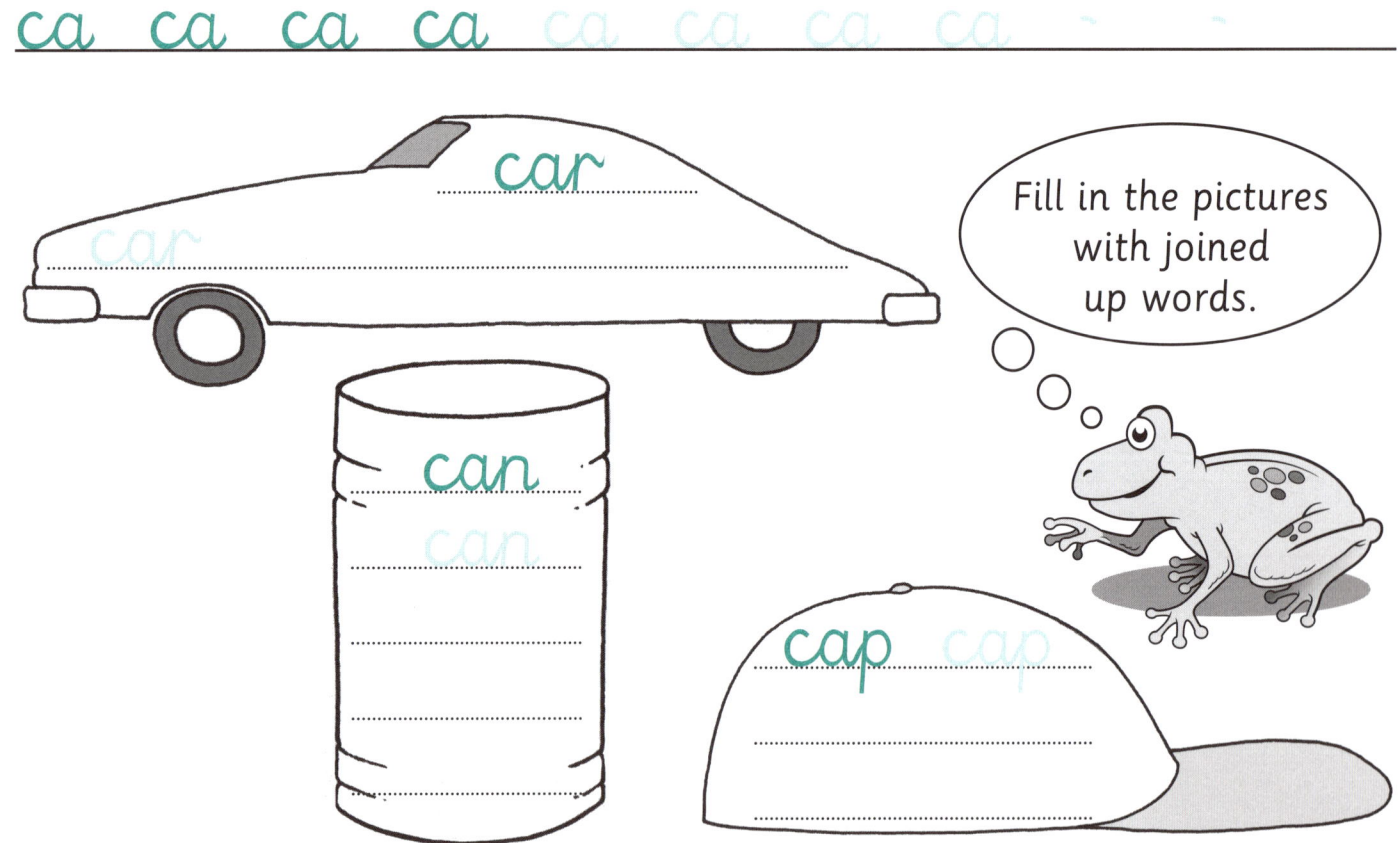

ca ca ca ca ca ca ca ca

car
car

can
can

cap cap

Fill in the pictures with joined up words.

6

Remember to make each letter the correct size.

Write each pair of letters before you dot the i.

in in in   im im im

is is is   ir ir ir

id id id   ip ip ip

Write the whole word and then put the dot on the i.

lip

lid

Join these pairs of letters.

ui   ui   ui

uc   uc   uc

ug   ug   ug

un   un   un

up   up   up

us   us   us

Complete the pictures.

cup

mug

8

Join these pairs of letters.

Remember which way the letter o goes.

ha ha ha   ho ho ho

hi hi hi   hu hu hu

he he he

Now try these words.

him him him him

her her her her

Look at these letters.

fo r v w

- ✱ Did you notice that the letters all finished at the top, except f which finishes with the line that goes across it?
- ✱ A join from any of these letters looks like a bridge, so we call it a bridge join.

Now try these.

on on on

or or or

oa oa oa

oo oo oo

Let's try some more bridge joins.

ri ri ri ri ri ri

ra ra ra ra ra ra

ru ru ru ru ru ru

ro ro ro ro ro ro

re re re re re re

Did you notice that each letter r was joined to a vowel?

Now let's join from v and w.

V W

va va va va   wa wa wa

vi vi vi vi   wi wi wi

ve ve ve ve   we we we

vu vu vu vu   wu wu

vo vo vo vo   wo wo wo

Did you notice that we didn't do the wu join many times?

Now we will try joining from the letter f.

Start here.

Join from here.

fi fi fi fi

fu fu fu fu

fo fo fo fo

fe fe fe fe

fe fi fo fum

Now we are going to do some more slope joins.

This time we will be joining to some tall letters.

Take great care.
Keep each letter the correct size.

al   al   al   al   al   al

el   el   el   el   el   el

Many words have double l.

ll   ll   ll   ll   ll   ll

Put words in the pictures.

wall   wall   wall

well

well

Try these pairs of letters...

...then complete the pictures.

Dot the *i* and cross the *t* after each pair is finished.

it it it it it it

et et et et et et

at at at at at at

cat

net

Copy these with care.

Keep each letter the correct size.

ut　ut　ut　ut　ut　ut

ct　ct　ct　ct　ct　ct

lt　lt　lt　lt　lt　lt

hut

Now complete the picture.

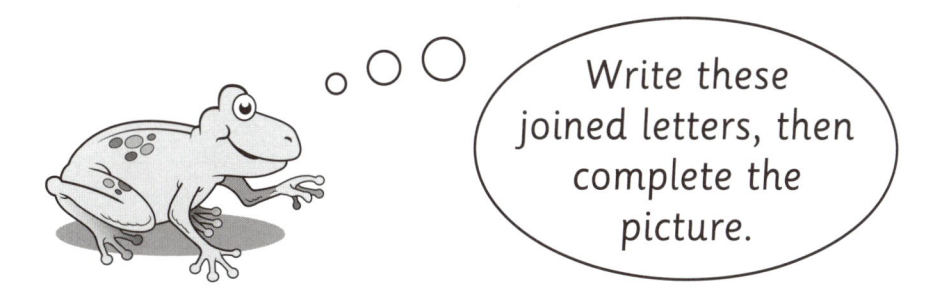

Write these joined letters, then complete the picture.

ab ab ab ab ab ab

eb eb eb eb eb eb

ib ib ib

ub ub ub

mb mb mb

crab

ch ch ch   th th th

uh uh uh   ah ah ah

eh eh eh   ih ih ih

church

Next we will try some bridge joins to tall letters.

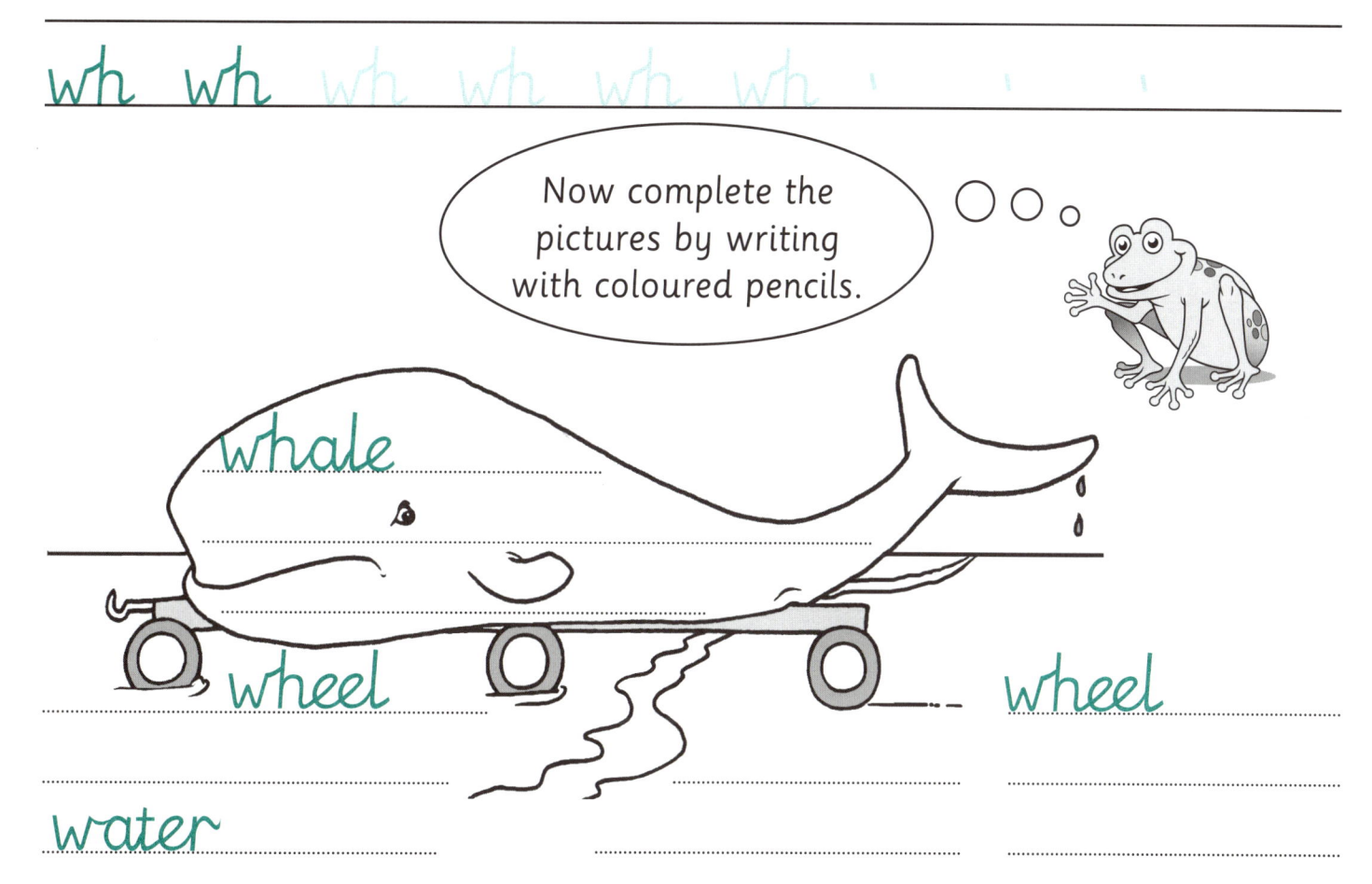

wh

wh wh wh wh wh wh

Now complete the pictures by writing with coloured pencils.

whale

wheel   wheel

water

19

Write these joins carefully... ...then complete the picture.

wl wl wl wl
wl

owl

rl rl rl rl

ol ol ol ol

Make the letter r carefully each time.

rb rb rb rb rb

rh rh rh rh rh

rt rt rt rt rt

ark

Complete the picture.

21

Here are some more pairs of letters.

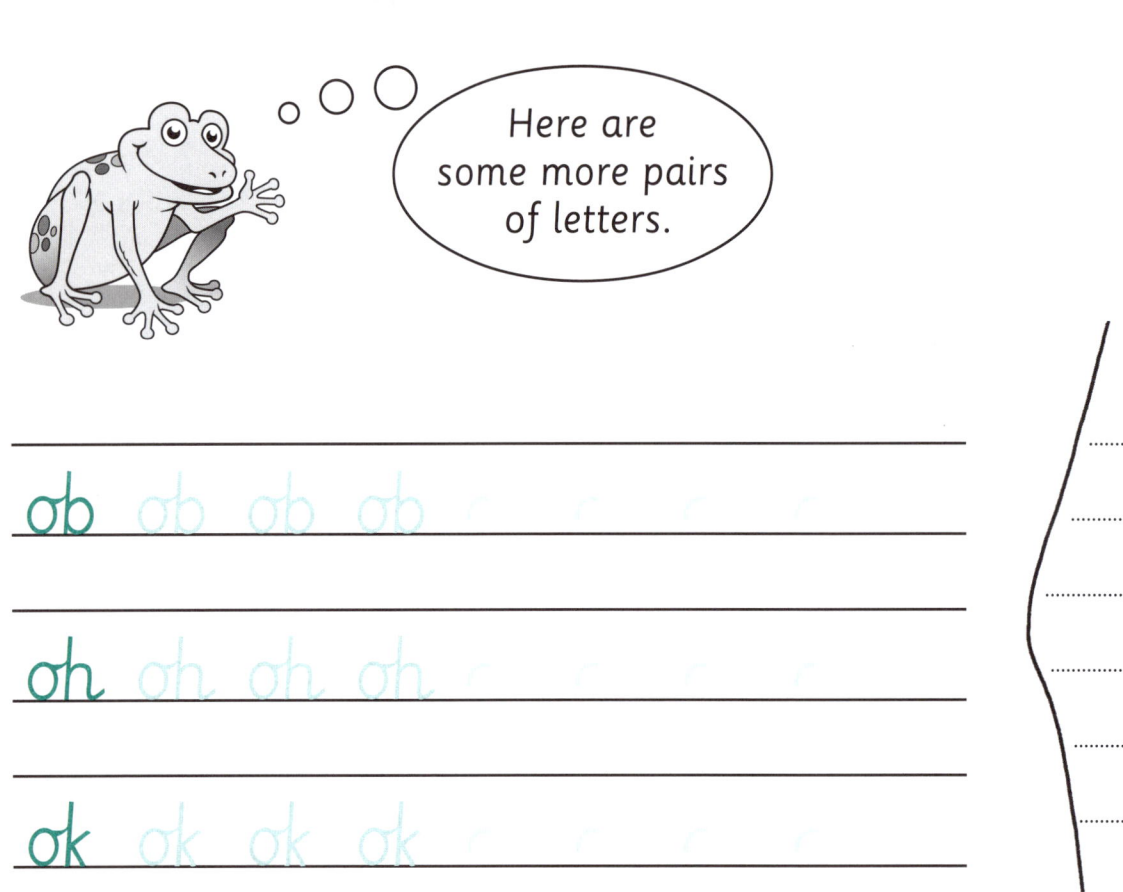

ob ob ob ob

oh oh oh oh

ok ok ok ok

ot ot ot ot

Write the words in the picture.

leg

foot

* On the next few pages you are going to write some words and sentences.
* Not all the letters are joined, so copy words very carefully.
* <u>Never</u> join a capital letter to the next one.

hill

Jack and Jill went up the hill.

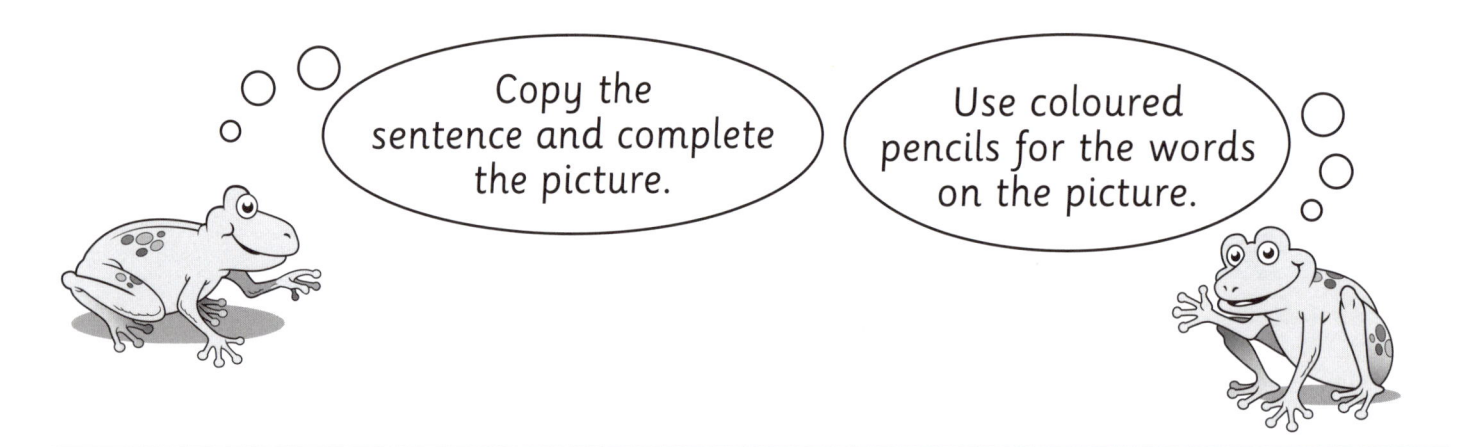

Copy the sentence and complete the picture.

Use coloured pencils for the words on the picture.

A blue van and a red car went along the road.

car

van

Fill the shapes in with words.

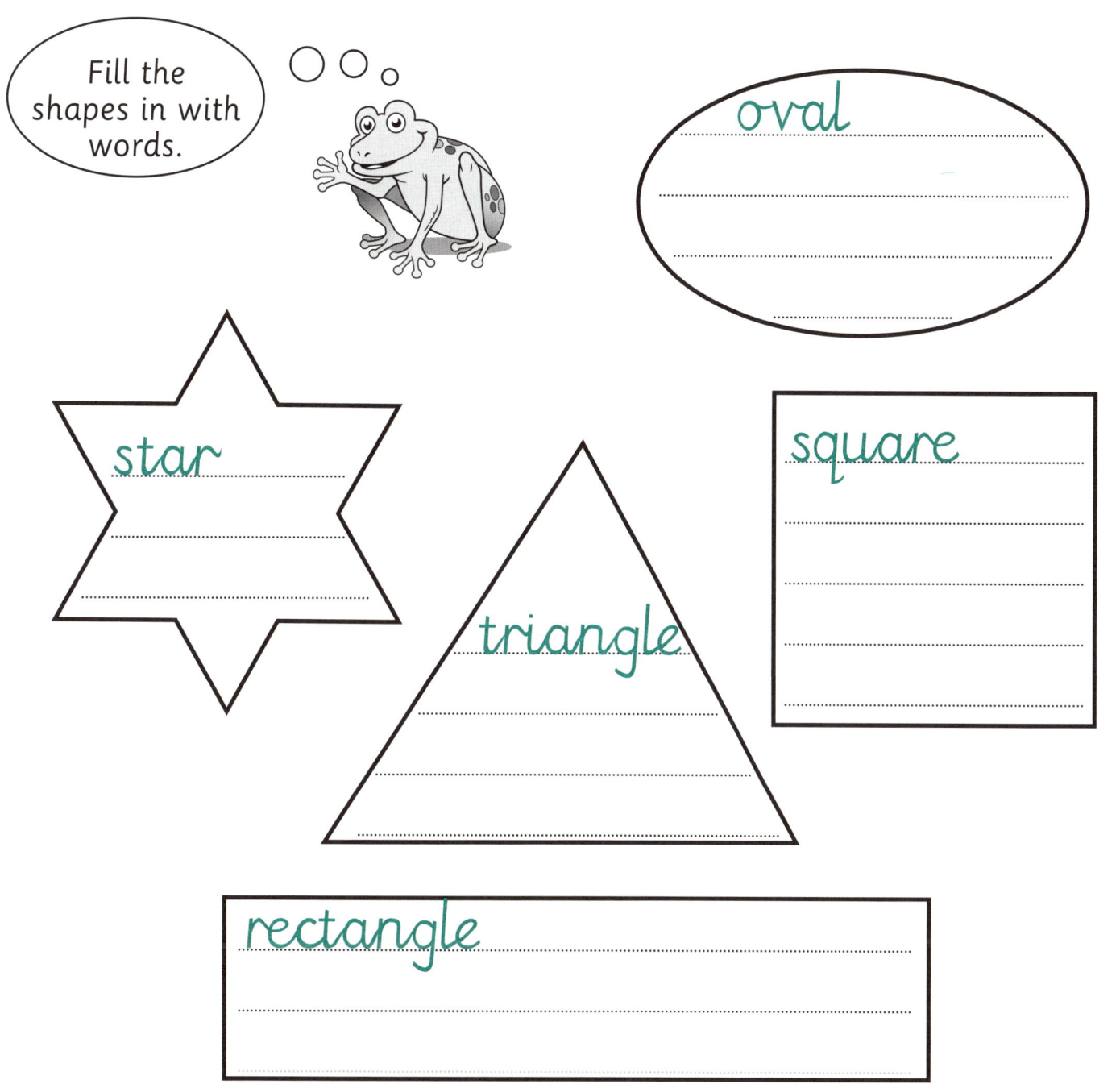

oval

star

square

triangle

rectangle

Ten parrots in a tall tree.

parrots

tree

Copy these words carefully.

They are words we write a lot.

who

what

where

when

why

which

Hickory Dickory Dock,

The mouse ran up the clock.

The clock struck one,

The mouse ran down,

Hickory Dickory Dock.

Do you know this rhyme?

clock

Mary had a little lamb.

Its writing was quite neat.

But when it tried to use a pen,

The ink spilled on its feet.

Look at these rhyming sentences and copy them.

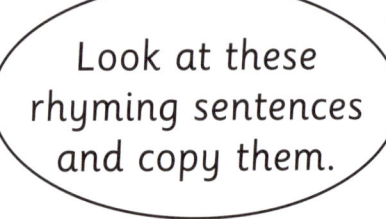

Use your neat joined writing in all your work.

A bear in a chair would give you a scare.

A rat in a hat looks silly like that.

Copy the sentence in your best joined writing.

There are five children around the

camp fire.

one
two
three
four
five
flames
wood

Now use coloured pencils to complete the picture.

Copy the sentence in your best joined writing.

"Don't cut my curls," he cried.

curls

chair

Now complete the picture. You may use coloured pencils.